# THE ROAD TO INVER

# The Road to Inver

*Translations, Versions, Imitations*
1975–2003
**TOM PAULIN**

To Tiffy
with every good wish
Tom Paulin

**ff**

*faber and faber*

First published in 2004
by Faber and Faber Limited
3 Queen Square London WIN 3AU
Published in the United States by Faber and Faber Inc.,
an affiliate of Farrar, Straus and Giroux LLC, New York

Photoset by RefineCatch Ltd, Bungay, Suffolk
Printed in England by T.J. International, Padstow, Cornwall

The right of Tom Paulin to be identified as author
of this work has been asserted in accordance with Section 77
of the Copyright, Designs and Patents Act 1988

A CIP record for this book
is available from the British Library

ISBN 0-571-22119-X

Acknowledgements
Some of these translations and versions have appeared in *Columbia:
A Journal of the Arts*, the *London Review of Books*, the *Times
Literary Supplement* and *West47*.
I have also drawn on previous volumes of mine: *A State of Justice,
Liberty Tree, Walking a Line, The Wind Dog, The Invasion Handbook,
The Riot Act* (a version of *Antigone* which was commissioned by the
Field Day Theatre Company), and *Seize the Fire* (a version of *Prometheus
Bound* which was commissioned by the Open University).
All these attempts are after, sometimes a long way after, the original
poems, a number of which I encountered in English translations.
I am grateful to Walid Khazendar for allowing me to publish
versions of three of his poems, and to Robin Bray for prose versions
of Khazendar's poems.
I am grateful to the National Endowment for Science,
Technology and the Arts for a fellowship – T.P.

2 4 6 8 10 9 7 5 3 1

For Sam and Liz Hynes

# Contents

vii

viii

# Oran
## (Camus)

The city itself, one has to admit, is ugly. It appears calm and quiet, but after some time the way it differs from many other centres of commerce becomes clear. Imagine – if that's possible – a town with no pigeons, no trees, no gardens, where you never hear the flusker of birds' wings, or even leaves rustling. A null, neutral place, where the changing seasons can only be told by looking up at the sky. A gentleness in the air tells you spring is coming – baskets of flowers brought in from the suburbs line the pavements. Spring is an opportunity for dozens of small businesses to fly their flags. During the summer the sun bakes the houses till they're like dry bones, and it smears their walls with an ashen dust. You can only live in the shadow of closed shutters. Then in the autumn mud pours from the sky. Good weather comes only in the winter months.

# The Island in the North Sea
## (Rilke)

Each farm squats inside a circular dam
like a fort a bawn a crater on the moon
bashed by storms each garden looks the same
and has it rough like an unloved orphan

who counts the bodies of drowned fishermen and grieves
as the islanders they keep indoors and stare
at crooked mirrors that show nicknames fancy things
among the delph that stacks each dresser

after tea some youth might take a dander
and rasp a tune on his harmonica
– its tacky girning he picked it up

in a foreign port some dockside bar
– then a sheep scumbles up a dyke a
gross hirpling dopey ominouslooking sheep

# The Cigarette
(Ponge)


Let's first try to catch the atmosphere – smoky, dry, tousled – no unkempt – that flows from the white or yellow cigarette poised just below this abyss that grows out of its tip.

Then let's try to see it as a person in its own right: a little torch, less luminous than perfumed, from which a finite number of tiny ash flakes are dropping in a rhythm that has yet to be determined.

Last thing, its passion: this burning button, peeling off its silver scales – a button sleeved by its most recent scales or flakes.

# The Albatross
## (Baudelaire)

Marilyn and the cassowary bird
– its head's protected by a bony helmet or casque –
they both know what the other bird's about
– idle gliding comrade of endless
voyages over tradescarred seas
where mariners counting the sea's clock
skrimshander whalebone or tempt him onto the deck
where with two left feet he paddles
on the dry boards – boards as stiff
as the ship's biscuit they chuck
at him – as well try swallow grey coke
or clinker – now some tar smoking a clay pipe takes
it and gives his long bony beak
– his glossy beak – a hard poke
another splays his feet out and hops
with as much grace as a sack
of old potatoes caked in mud
then laughs at the poor craychur he's mocking
– yes we know that the poet any star like Marilyn
and the cassowary too resemble the albatross
– whole crowds rough as those jack
tars squatting on sunscrubbed boards yak
away at them all – then with gossip and innuendo
– how they roll their tongues on the name *Monroe* –
they lay each in turn on their back
and rip out their guts

# The Storm
## (Montale)

The hard leaves on the magnolia
they're ruffled by thunder
then thumped by hailstones

(crystal and archaic the sounds
that chink in your nocturnal cabinet
and that grain of sugar
– a tiny lump of sleep yolk
stuck in your eyelid's shell
is all that's left of the gilt
inlay on mahogany
on badly scuffed leather bindings)

then the lightning makes trees and walls
famous for a moment
– marble a grain of manna
discandied I mean destroyed
– oh it's carved inside you
sister that sermon
you preach against me
it ties us closer than love can
– now the rude crash quiver
of timbrels (tumbrils I nearly said)
over the black ditch
then the fandango's yukky clatter

5

and some gesture that gropes or teases
– a little trailing capillary
                    as you turned you pushed
your smoky hair with one hand
and waved roughly with the other
                    then the darkness pitched on you

# Belongings
## (Khazendar)


Who entered my room when I was out
and moved the vase on the mantelpiece just a tad?
who skewed that print – a Crusader – on the far wall?
and those pages loose on my desk
they're a shade dishevelled aren't they?

of course someone's read them
and my pillow's never been dented this way
– not by any lovely head
that stray shirt I'd never leave on the floor
– some shit's dropped it

so who came into my room? who?
and who'll put the vase back exactly
as it was? who'll
straighten the mailed knight in his corner?
and who'll restore to my shirt and pillow
their full rights as citizens
of my single room?

# Don't
(Heine)

Don't mention it ever
– not when we're lying in bed
or eating dinner
– not when I'm making a meal
of your wet cunt
don't mention Deutschland to me

all that's been written and said
about homeland family slums
– I've gone right the way through it
so don't tell me I want to go back
– all the cards are there on the table
but the table's a long way away

we're just taking a holyer
for the rest of our natural lives
– like a tight big apple
we'll eat up ourselves and this city
so don't mention the skyblue Rhine
or that gospel tribe in the oakgrove

# Unavoidable
## (Goethe)

Who can say to the birds
*shut the fuck up*
or tell the sheep in the yow trummle
not to struggle and leap?

you think there's no manners on me
when I act like a lout
but it's the shearer who tugs at me
– that's what it's about

who can stop me chucking words
onto this heavenly white page?
– Hafiz it's such a struggle
being in love at my age

# The Skeleton
(Verlaine)


Two pachles both stocious are lurching back
over a battlefield – they're doubles of our old friend
the miles gloriosus and they look bulky like sacks
so maybe they're Hessians who like Jack Falstaff
are – mortal men sir – full of sack
and sorry the war has staggered to an end
but then they see this gnawed daft
– nit of a translator says *deboned* – skeleton
lying there among the puddles and shellholes
the mud the debris the bust or abandoned weapons
– like a trapdoor its mouth gapes open
as it lies there static a bleached symbol of ending
then Captain Bones cranks up and addresses our two
squaddies
– more to come – tell the ranks – more great more
dulce days!

# The Coastguard Station
## (Montale)

Henry Snodden and me we've nearly forgotten
that scraggy coastguard station –
a ruin from the Black and Tan war
it stood on Tim Ring's hill above the harbour
like an empty a crude roofless barracks
– same as the station in Teelin or Carrick
with the usual concrete harbour
like a berm built the century before last
to make a new fishing village with a slightly daft
name – in this case Portnoo – below the head

one August we came back and instead
of that ruin there was only the grassy track
on the grassy hill and so the field's stayed
year after year though we're both afraid
that one day very soon that unused field
'll be sold as sites – then we'll watch
as a new little colony of thatched
breezeblock cottages – *Irish Holiday Homes*
with green plastic oilgas tanks at the back –
as a new colony starts up all owned
by people like us from Belfast
who've at last laid that claggy building's ghost
– well I wouldn't go as far as that

# To a Political Poet
### (Heine)


Your baggy lyrics,
they're like a cushion
stuffed with smooth grudges
and hairy heroes.

'Me Mam's Cremation,'
'Me Rotten Grammar School',
'Ode to the Toffee-Nosed Gits
Who Mocked My Accent'.

Now your whinges
get taught in class
and the kids feel righteous –
righteous but cosy.

# Last Statement
## (Mayakovsky)

It's after one,
you're in the sack, I guess.
the stars are echoed
in the Volga's darkness
and I'm not fussed
or urgent anymore.
I won't be writing you
my slogans and my kisses
in daft capitals:
we bit green chillies
and we're through.
We were like lovers
leaning from a ferry
on the White Canal –
our arguments statistics,
our fucks and cries
notched on the calculus.
Ack, the night has jammed
each signal from the stars,
and this, this is my last
stittering, grief-splintered
call-sign to the future.
Christ, I want to wow
both history and technology . . .
I could tell it to the world right now.

# The Pleasures of the Door
(Ponge)


Kings don't touch doors.

They never know this happiness: to push one of those grand familiar panels in front of you – push it gently or boldly – then turn round and let it snick back into place. Yes, you can hold a door in your arms.

You feel happy as you grip in your palm – grip all in one go – the little porcelain knob or navel on the belly of one of those tall obstacles. It's a sudden hand-to-hand encounter, then that little glitch on the threshold, as the eye opens and your whole body gladly takes possession of its new apartment.

Your friendly hand holds onto the knob, before giving it a decisive shove that shuts you in – the click of that strong, well-oiled lock is most reassuring.

# The Lagan Blackbird
### (Irish)

The wee blackbird settles
in a whin bush
on the slope of the hill
then opens
its yolkyellow bill
– now its fresh
song lifts up and fills
the sky over Belfast Lough

## My Name
### (Akhmatova)

Tatar coarsegrained
it came from nowhere my name
and it sticks
aye sticks like a burr
to any disaster
– no it is disaster

# Chorus
## (from *Antigone*)

There are many wonders on this earth
and man has made the most of them;
though only death has baffled him
he owns the universe, the stars,
*sput* satellites and great societies.

Fish pip inside his radar screens
and foals kick out of a syringe:
he bounces on the dusty moon
and chases clouds about the sky
so they can dip on sterile ground.

By pushing harder every way,
by risking everything he loves,
he makes us better day by day:
we call this progress and it shows
we're damned near perfect!

# Darkness at Noon
### (Nerval)


Anyone who stares hard at the sun
sees a dot in front of their eyes a little smut
that jeuks about like a white bat

– look when I was a bold youngster
it was glory – call it Parnassus – I stared at
till I saw a jerky wee spot

ever since like a full stop or a bit of crepe
when my eye stops
I see it stuck there – a skift a skelf a smear

between myself and perfect happiness
– only the eagle who's without fear
basks on the brassy mountain happy and glorious

# From the Death Cell
## (Chénier)


We live – dishonoured, in the shit. So what? It had to be.
  This is the pits and yet we feed and sleep.
Even here – penned in, watered and waiting for the chop
  (just place your bets) – affairs take off,
there's gossip, bitching and a pecking-order.
  Songs, jokes, card-schools: she lifts her skirts; someone
bops a tight balloon against the window-panes.
  It's like the speeches of those seven hundred eejits
(Barrère's the shiftiest of the lot) – a comic fart
  we whoop and cheer and then forget.
One jumps, another skips; that greasy pack
  of gut and gullet politicians raps and hoots
until, dead quick, the door scrakes open
  and our tiger-masters' wee pimp struts in.
Who's getting it today? We freeze and listen,
  then all but one of us knows it isn't him . . .

# Emulation
(Goethe)


Your kind of verse is what I'm after
– *repeat that repeat* those little rills or runs
that turn into *repeat this this* before
they pitch and split – they don't stumble – you know that

your song it travelled out through desert space
and touched this German heart – a heart
that was nowhere near indifferent
– then like someone trying to count in Latin
I looked up and saw your different numbers

# The Poem as Monument
## (Horace, *Odes* III.30)

Tougher than bronze much taller – more pointed –
than any pyramid my poems they aren't
to be tossed by war by the north wind or
drowned in a flood – no the years O they won't
kick them in a ditch or rub my name out
– whenever priests and Vesta's holy virgins
design a ritual pause a hush
my fame will be visible on that hill
our Capitol like a green bush
it'll reach dingy rainstung coasts
– dreary towns west of the Bann –
till my cadences they stretch and sing
in coarse or homely tongues all
better for the Greek rhythms and metres
that I a former slave's son
brought into our blocky language making
it more decorous pungent glossy sweeter
like this garland on my forehead – Apollo's laurel

# Prologue
## (Langland)

*for Andrew McNeillie*

One summer's morning in the white the soft the widening
sunshine I struggled like a daft sheep into a
shepherd's smock a ragged thing – stained and greasy –
that made me look like a rude a houseless hermit who's
up to no good as he wanders out all hunched up
toward the wide the crowded world there to witness
– bear witness –
to all its wonders and atrocities
– ack that May morning on the Malvern hills
I happened on the strangest sight
– I was foundered and wanted just to shut my eyes
and sleep on the bank of a burn where I lay me down
looking at the water sliding softly by me
till I went – where was it? – into a wilderness
where I saw high in the East a huge tower
standing on a hill against the sun a valley
under it with a prison no a blockhouse a claggy
blockhouse hemmed in by ditches black and still as it was
and from it came screams – highpitched steely screams –
jagged in the throats of men being dragged through a heavy
    catechism
– men whose houses had been knocked to the ground
in villages with weak wells or no wells at all
– between the tower and the abyss there was a field
spread out like a cloth and busy with all kinds of folk
rich ones and the poor who worked hard sowing and
    ploughing
and winning from the earth all that gets wasted

or made into fine clothes that turn people proud
others though pray and do penance for the love of God
in the hopes of living in heaven for ever
just as hermits anchor themselves in their cells
instead of dandering about like brave lads
looking for lips to stick their tongues and dicks in
– others turned to trade and did much better
still others sang and made music so coins showered
into their guiltless caps but jokers jeuked
through the crowd – they're the children of Judas
and could work if they wanted for they're clever they're
    dead cunning
but he as St Paul says he who talks filth
serves the devil just like those tramps and beggars
who pretend to be drunk then get real drunk and angered
or doze off stocious in the middle of an oath
– there were pilgrims too and palmers who
had travelled together to Rome and to Compostela
and brought back either wise stories or yarns
you couldn't believe for a minute though they'd repeat
them over and over all their lives long
– some I saw had gone out looking for holy saints
but their tongues were tempered like metal scrap metal were
    beaten
flat by the lies they told till the clack
of their speech had one catch then another
like their hooked staves on the way to Walsingham
– their women followed after these big beefy lubbers
who'd get themselves up in clerical dress
to make the others feel small so very very small
– friars I happened on from all the four orders
preaching long sermons so they could fill their bellies
they did their own thing with the gospels

– embroidered all those stories like their fancy copes
prophets making a profit for charity's long
gone into business – now it shrives lords or ladies
by the dozen – odd things have happened here these
last few years and unless and until these
fat friars mend their quarrel with Holy Church
there'll be such mischief such evil let loose in the world
– I heard a pardoner reciting a sermon
and just like a priest he brought out a bull sealed
by a bishop – it gave him the power the
plenary power to absolve anyone from broken fasts and broken vows – course the common people
they loved him and relished his speech they
crawled up on their knees to kiss his bull
while he bonked them with his breviary
then raked in their rings and brooches
with his rolledup parchment his stiff scroll
– they give their hearts to lecherous thieves and if
the bishop were worthy and kept his ears open
his seal would never be sent out to con the people
but this rogue he doesn't preach with the bishop's permission
– the parish priest and the pardoner they split the takings
that but for them would go to the poor of the parish
rectors and parish priests complained to the bishop
that their parishes were poor since the plague-time
they begged a licence and leave to live in London
where they would sell themselves for silver sweet silver
bishops and BAs doctors of divinity
who're charged under Christ with the care of souls
who wear the tonsure as sign they should shrive their flocks
preach to them pray for them and feed the poor
they stay all Lent in London and out of Lent too
some serve the king by checking figures or by claiming

what's owed from wardships waived estates
vacant houses with no heir sturgeons washed on the sea
  shore
while others serve lords and ladies manage households
gabble mass and matins with no spirit no devotion – no
  religion–
– Christ I fear will curse many of these men
on Judgement Day for I can see the power
Peter had to bind and unbind as the Book says
and how he too at our Lord's command made
love the centre – love shared between the four
greatest virtues we call cardinal – meaning
hinges that open and shut the gates that
lead to heavenly life or down to hell
but those other cardinals in Rome who've
taken the same name and the power to make popes
as well as the power Peter had – no I won't impugn
those men only note that electing a pope it asks for
love and learning – I could say more I could go on
about the papal court but it's not my place
– and then a king guided by knights came into the field
the might yes might of the common people it gave
him sovereign power but Common Sense it came after
and created advisers – then the king the knights the clergy
they all decreed that the common people should look after
  them
so the common folk they got together and
invented all the different trades their gear their tackle their
  trim
– ploughmen they hired to till the soil
for the common good while Common Sense he or she
helped the king and the people to shape the law
and root it – root us – in loyalty so each man and woman

knew dead on where their rights and their duties lay
– then this lean screggy loon he stuck his head up
and knelt before the king all the while speaking
in a priestly a most smarmy orotund bowelly fashion
– was he perhaps taking the piss?
– Christ keep your majesty and all your kingdom safe
and may your fair and just – your equal – rule be rewarded
in heaven and in the love of your subjects your
loyal subjects – then from out a blue sky
an angel leaned down and spoke precisely in Latin
these folk had no learning so they couldn't
argue or speak for themselves – they could only suffer
– suffer and serve –
then the angel said you announced you're king a prince
but in time you may be neither – it's your duty then
to make the laws of Christ the King work as they ought
– be mild and be just make sure you clothe justice
with mercy and sow only those crops you hope to reap
but if you strip justice bare of mercy
you'll be judged by justice alone – plant mercy
and you shall harvest mercy – then a joker
a word muncher a boker answered the angel
– since a king's only a king by the act
of ruling his people he's an empty name
if he doesn't maintain the laws
then the common people – they wished to chuck in
their mite of advice – the people cried out in Latin
to the king – let him make what he could of it –
to us the king's decrees are as binding as the laws
– just then a scour of rats mice in their nimbling hundreds
bunched quick in a conference for a common purpose
because a court cat would come when he wanted
and bite their bums and knock them about a bit

– we daren't go on we're that terrified of him
and if we girn at his games he'll grab us by the neck
till we loathe this life and cry to be rid of it
but if we use our wits and stand up firm to him
we could live like lords and rest easy
– a big powerful rat famous for miles round
put forward this policy in a slick speech
– I've seen men he said in the city of London
going about with spick collars and neat necklaces on them
they've no leads and can walk where they like – anyplace
coney warrens waste ground common land –
other places too at certain times I hear tell
but it strikes me by Christ that those boys had better each
have a bell on his collar
then we'd know where they were and could run if we
    wanted
it's clear to me we should buy a bell
– a brass or a silver one chank and shiny –
stick it to a collar and clip it on the cat's neck
then we can hear if he's running or resting or chasing
    around
in a good mood is he? – we can come out and play then –
but if he gets nasty we can skip off quick
the whole congress of rats agreed this good plan
but when a bell had been bought and clipped to a collar
there wasn't one rat in the whole worried crowd
would dare run out and tie it to the cat's neck
we're all scared they sighed our work's wasted
– a mouse a most sensible mouse I thought
pushed up front and fed these words to the rats
– if we killed the cat another'd come to annoy us
so I say to our people best let him alone
seven years since my father said this to me

– where the cat's just a kitten the court is in chaos
it's there in the scriptures if you'll heed the preacher
     *Vae terri ubi puer rex est, etc.*
at night no one can rest for fear of the rats
so let's be fair while he's out after rabbits
we needn't fear for our skins – it's game he feeds on
better a little loss than a long sorrow
though we kicked that tyrant out there'd be worse trouble
we mice would munch many tons of good malt
and you rats'd rip the clothes off men's backs
if that cat wasn't there to walk all over you
there'd be a right rat mess for you'll never rule yourselves
don't cross the cat or the kitten ever – that's my advice
all this talk about collars is total crap –
let the cat jump where he wants when he wants
my motto is this we're all individuals so let's
each one chase his own interests and be done
with this gassing in groups it's getting us nowhere
– what this dream of mine means or what its message is
the critics can tell when they lift their eyes from the text

*

– in this assembly I saw so many trolls in puffed costumes
a hundred men in silk suits they swayed there like corn
barristers all making speeches and entering pleas
for the fattest fees they could get but they never
once opened their mouths for the love of our Lord
you might as soon measure mist on the Malvern hills
as get a word out of them if they couldn't
see your coins on the table – many more men
in this assembly I saw – bakers flabby bakers excellent
    brewers
great big butchers excellent smiths wool websters

linen weavers tailors tinkers tollmen
masons and coal miners and many others
all those who lived by the fruit of their craft
dykemen and diggers too who do their work badly
tell dirty jokes and sing bawdy songs all day
while cooks cried hot pies! hot pies!
fat pigs! fat geese! come eat! come eat!
barmen and pub landlords they called wine!
red wine white wine wine from Alsace
Flemish and wine from Rochelle they'll soothe
the roast in your belly – all this and much more
I saw in my sleep on soft grass in soft
sunshine by a running river in the Malvern hills

# Contemplation 27
## (Hugo)

Really because we hate them
I try to love the spider and the nettle
– the nettle has a hairy stem
– no *hairy stalk* would be better
and the spider has wire legs
brisk and bent below a body
like a tiny egg
– nothing but nothing fulfils
and everything punishes
their mournful hope
– they're damned dreggy meagre
so one might as well
love a piece of old rope
– like grey underpants
they carry the stain of the provincial
and can find nobody
to admire their vernacular
they're wee victims
of nature and history
who bring a taste of some minor abyss
bring grot and gloom
– ack they're like shattered limbs
or the shut smell of piss
in a basement room

# The Rooks
## (Rimbaud)

When the ground's as hard as rock
and the Angelus has gone dead
in each crushed village
Lord let the rooks
– those great clacky birds
sweep down from the clouds
onto fields and ridges

floppy crowd that bursts
into stony cries
the wind's bashing your nests!
– along yellow rivers roads
with their pitted Calvaries
over ditches and holes
you must scatter and rally!

turn in your thousands
over the fields of France
where the recent dead
lie maimed and broken
– in your clattery dance
our black funereal bird
remind us how they bled!

you sky saints in the treetops
draped on that dusky mast
above paradise lost

please let the May songbirds be
– for our sake who're trapped
beaten servile unfree
in the hawthorns' green dust.

# André Chénier
## (Tsvetayeva)

André Chénier climbed up the ladder.
What a sin to be alive!
Iron, iron and cordite, these days
And a burnt tenor.

What father would cut the collar
From his son's shirt?
There are times the daylight's a quick terror
And no one living looks quite human.

4 April 1918

# The Pipe
(Mallarmé)


Yesterday I was dreaming idly of a long evening's labour at my desk – fine winter work – when I happened on my old pipe. I chucked a packet of cigarettes in the wastebin: they belonged to past summers, to boyish pleasures, leafshadow, muslin dresses that smell like white bread. Then I took up my sturdy pipe like the serious scholar I am, a man who wants a long unbothered smoke in order to get down to work. But I never guessed what a surprise my old mate – he'd been shunned – had in store for me. One puff and I'd forgotten all the baggy epics that were still to be written, for the astonishing thing was that last winter breathed right in my face. I hadn't lifted my cherry briar – it had that bygone look – since returning to France, and now the whole of London, London as I'd lived it and walked its streets a year back, gave itself to me there in my study. First, the dear dirty fogs that get right inside your head till you feel them chill and tacky on the surface of your brain – those fogs, they have a thick smell that's all their own, especially when they creep in through a loose window frame. My tobacco smelt of a room darkened by leather armchairs and a bulgy sofa, all with a scurf of coal dust over them, a scrawny black cat purring on the knitted cushion. O the large-hearted fires! and the maid with muscly arms rattling the coal scuttle – the scumble of those black lumps on the metal grate in the morning, just as the postman goes *bok! bok!* like a uni-formed copper on the front door, and brings me back to life. Once again I was looking through the window at those dying trees in the deserted square. I saw the Channel unravel – I'd crossed it so often that winter, soaked and shivering on the bridge, sooty with the smoke from the funnel. Beside my poor lost loved one in her long dress, grey as road dust, a damp cloak on her frozen shoulders, a straw hat without a feather and only one tatty ribbon – the sort of hat posh women discard the moment they arrive home, and my poor dear retrims for another journey. Her bonnet looked a mess in the salt sea air, and round her neck was the terrible stained handkerchief we wave when we say goodbye for the very last time.

# Winter Becoming Spring
### (Horace, *Odes* 1.4)

Tight winter, it slacks off. A spring breeze
In from the west makes a pleasant change.
Dry keels are winched down the strand.
Stalled cattle, men by their firesides, are restless
Now stiff frosts sheet the fields no longer.

Enter Venus, fresh from her island retreat,
Leading a lovely band of Nymphs and Graces
Below a huge moon: the earth trembles
Under their flickering feet, while deep underground
Vulcan sweats at his blazing boilers.

It's the in-thing now to grease your hair back,
Garland it with glossy myrtles
Or the first flowers earth has unfurled.
In the dark woods you should sacrifice a lamb
To Faunus, or a kid if it suits him.

Pale-faced Death is a great democrat,
Evicting the poor man from his slum
And the peer from his stately home.
Life's much too short, my dear Sestius,
For the big ambitions, the distant prospects.

Night and the ghosts of dead heroes close in;
That one cramped cell – all we're allowed – is ready:
There'll be no more drinking there, no boy to fancy.
Here and today he sets the young men on fire,
Soon the girls will start burning for him too.

# Bournemouth
(Verlaine)

The fir trees twist down as far as the shore
– a narrow wood of firs, laurels, pines.
Disguised as a village, the town hides out
in these evergreens – red brick chalets,
then the white villas of the bathing stations.

The inky wood drops down from a heath, a plateau;
comes, goes, scoops out a small valley, then climbs,
   greenblack,
before turning into douce groves that hold the light –
it lays gold on the shaded, sleepylooking graveyard
which slopes in steeped stages, laidback, insouciant.

To the left a heavy tower – it has no spire –
squats above the church that's hidden by the trees.
That hard basic tower, the wooden jetty in the distance,
are Anglicanism – brisk, bossy, heartless,
and utterly without hope.

It's the kind of moment I like best
– neither mist nor sunshine, but the sun guessed
from the dissolving mist that melts like a dancer,
as the creamy sky turns pink before it goes.
The air gleams like a pearl, the sea's gold, pure gold.

The protestant tower brangs out a single note,
then two three four, then a batch of eight
pealing out like floating feathers.

37

Eager, joyous, sad, reproachful,
the metal music's gold, then bronze, then fire.

Huge but so mild, it coats the narrow wood,
this beautiful sound that travels slowly
over the sea – the sea appears to sing and tremble
the way a road dings and thuds under the boots
of a battalion marching towards the front.

Then the sound poem's over. But the madder light
drops onto the sea in thick gobbets like sobs
– a cold sunset, another New Year,
a bloodstained town that quivers there in the west
and wears the darkness like a skewed crown.

The evening digs in, icecold, the slatted jetty
vibrates, and the wind in the wood lashes out
and sings as it whips – a cascade of blows
like the hammerbrash of all I've done wrong
– my sins, my betrayals, the people I've hurt.

I'm heartsick, lonely, my soul's a void.
The sea and the winter winds fight it out.
Like a bankrupt actor, I shout out old lines
and turn the night into ambush, catastrophe,
a smell of greasepaint and cheap evil.

Three chimes now, like three notes on a flute
Three more! three more! it's the Angelus
out of catholic England that says: Peace now,
the Word is made flesh so your sins can be forgiven,
a virgin's womb has quickened, the world is free.

So God speaks through the voice of *His* chapel
– it's halfway up the hill, on the edge of the wood.
Mother Church, Rome, a cry, a gesture,
that calls me back to that one happiness
and makes the rebel bow before the Cross and listen.

The night strokes me, the forgotten jetty
falls silent under the mounting tide.
Luckily there's a straight track marked out
that'll take me home – like a child I hurry
through a wood that's as dark and scary as the Black Forest.

# L'Anguilla
## (Montale)

Northern muscle the eel
– greyblack all slimy
it flexes through our warm sea
our rivers and estuaries
then licks their bottoms
with its tongue its slime
tongue threading each muddy bum
– it likes shifting labyrinths
but it aims for the red granite
flicking its slick inches
snaking and thinning
an oiled slippy whip
cracking up and up
as the chestnut blossoms
burst white over its worm's
eye view inside the bosom
of dead water where this sperm
– tail and fins fletched
like love's arrow
in a ditch
in that dry or wet –
either way hairy – slit
where this sperm always fits
– a wee tiny bomb
kissing the ovum
then going *boom!*
in the palmy womb
this wet spark

burns green in the dark
only to break
and chitter in the wind dog's arc
over cities made desolate
– burnt out by hate
till its glister
coils moistly in the iris
like brother and sister
joined in perfect vision
– then it bolts again
your fleshy slate
pencil – turns itself and nature around
warming the muddy ground

(Taormina, October 2001)

## Symbolum
(Goethe)


The mason lives
in this or that street
and all his actions
are like yours or mine.
He makes us equal.

He sees loose clouds
like a bishop's jowls
and the furred stars
that should be even –
king superstitions.

But he'll go out
with spirit-level,
square and trowel
to plant a ladder
on this earth.

The sun shines
on his foundations –
a pentagram
cut in packed soil,
the bricks stacked ready.

# Le Crapaud
## (Corbière)

An airless night a sort of song
– moon a metal plaque
its tattery shadows inky green
. . . buried alive under those laurel roots
the song's a slimy echo pulsing pulsing
– he shuts up – look he's down by the drain
– a toad! his pursy skin pubbles
but I'm guarding him with my own skin
– look at him – a wingless poet bald as a coot
a mud nightingale a singing turd
. . . he starts his song again *yuk yuk yuk*
why'm I disgusted? see the light in his eyes
no – he flubs under some mooncold rubble

night night – fat Mr Turd he's me

# Voronezh

(Akhmatova)

You walk on permafrost
in these streets.
The town's silly and heavy
like a glass paperweight
stuck on a desk –
a wide steel one
glib as this pavement.
I trimp on ice,
the sledges skitter and slip.
Crows are crowding the poplars,
and St Peter's of Voronezh
is an acidgreen dome
fizzing in the flecked light.
The earth's stout as a bell –
it hums like that battle
on the Field of Snipes.
Lord let each poplar
take the shape of a wine-glass
and I'll make it ring
as though the priest's wed us.
But that tin lamp
on the poet's table
was watched last night –
Judas and the Word
are stalking each other
through this scroggy town
where every line has three stresses
and only the one word, *dark*.

# The Velléda
(Verlaine)


I pushed the dodgy gate into the garden
– warmed by the sun and at ease
I strolled over the grass
as the dew shook its hard bright splinters

it was all the same – the vines the arbour
the rattan chairs the fountain
svelte and slivery like the way the aspen
leaves were shivering their chaff their tinsel

the roses swayed the lilies stood there
upright like nuns or soldiers
as the larks spilt their songs

I found the Velleda – it too hadn't changed
but its plaster was flaky a tad strange
like the smell of mignonette stinging the air

# The Emigration of the Poets
### (Brecht)

Homer belonged nowhere
and Dante he'd to leave home
as for Tu Fu and Li Po
they did a flit through the smoke
– 30 million were no
more in those civil wars
while the high courts
tried stuff Euripides under the floor
and even Shakespeare got a gagging order
as he lay dying in Stratford
– Villon who wrote 'Les Pendus'
had visits from the Muse
and from the Beast
– i.e. the police
though at least Lucretius
was nicknamed *Le bien aimé*
and slipped away from *Heim*
just like Heine
– now watch me here Bertolt Brecht
I'm a pike
shtuck in this Danish thatch.

# Sea Wind
## (Mallarmé)


It's a sad creature I'm afraid the body
all the classics – every book that stands steady
on my shelves I've read them through but only
to make this wish – oh to walk to the edge of the sea
and watch stints skittering along the tideline
then scattering up and beyond into the sky!
not a thing – not the gardens of mouldy chateaus
wet and glaucous in her eyes –
not a thing no one will stop me I've got to go
down to the wild sea – I tell you not nights
crossing blank pages under my desklamp
– not that desert wild or the sigh
of a dumpy girl breastfeeding her child
will stop me booking a berth on some tramp
steamer heaving its rust toward the tropics

– I'll wave my snotrag from the deck sick
of stroking my own boredom – by the saltstained
     smokestack
let me dream of wind and wrecks!

# Love Thy Neighbour
## (Jacob)

You've clocked him – wee crap-o
a toad trying
to flup across a street
on the edge of town
like a rag doll
– he's on his knees
maybe he's ashamed?
– no not at all
he's rheumatic he's
dragging one leg
where's he going with that stiff
it looks like an extra leg?
– he's crawled out of the gutter
poor fool poor clown
– no he's a lucky chancer
no one has noticed him
just the way no one used notice me
when I walked down the same street
now the children they laugh at my yellow star
– lucky toad! you don't wear a yellow star

## *from* Algerian Diary
(Sereni)


He's flying high now
– he's out of it – on wings –
the first soldier to hit
which beach in Normandy?
and fall flat
I know it because someone touched
me on the shoulder and whispered
ever so gently
*pray for Europe our Europe*
just as that steel Armada
was bunching up to the coast of France

halfasleep I replied
it's the wind's frappy sound
only that
but if really and truly
you were the first to fall down
on that beach
– was it Arromanches? –
you must try if you can
to say a prayer
for I'm dead
both to the war and the peace
– the music I hear
is a flapflack as the guy-ropes
they beat against the tentpoles
and the stretched canvas
– it's not the music of angels in heaven

but for me
under this red canvas cross
it's all the music I'll get
– like a crutch or a grudge
long years in the nursing
it's my basic
my only ration

Hospital Camp 127, June 1944

# The Caravans on Lüneburg Heath
### (Dach)

one of those unlucky Fridays Simon
    a bust-up dirty time to be alive
writing an elegy for the pumpkin hut and *Gärtchen*
without your neat metre and full rhymes

what I have to say's dead obvious
    we've had x years of blood and shit
    and some of us have written poems
    or issued too many credos through the press

    *Simplex plays the pipe indeed*
    *But the soldiers pay no heed.*

waiting a contact watching the normals
in the quick frame of their street lives
. . . cigarette butts carriers bus passes ackhello
they lie whole weeks in attics
wire potato clamps
or kit themselves in aprons and straw hats
knowing the natural order
for the vigilant fake it is

I'm watching three young butchers
dressed up as themselves
it's a hot new lunchtime
in the town of Newry
they camp through the market – look

then break triangulate gap

you'll hear the shots like instant recollection

*Simplex sees the squad car stop –*
*Four young men have got the chop.*

\*

it took us a few years only to grow that house
on a bit of land the town council give us
a cultured place beside the River Pregel
where we read out poems to each other
hoping that Zion's daughter
was maybe a presence in our speech
– surely she'd help us shelter from the rain?

other people that concept we grew up with
they made us out a pack of tubes
our heads full of gourds pumpkins squashes peppers
we treated cucumbers like art objects
and loved the slippy gunge that cauls the melon seeds
every stranger was made welcome in our house
you brought a bottle or a spondee and got tight
you cast your bread upon the waters of the Pregel
and things came back to you that primal happiness
before you turned like Christ upon the mother
sangar blockhouse lookout post OP
you made a garden in its place
a cultivated man turning the earth and raking soil
till it smells like new cord and you press the seeds in

\*

Simon you're the It that isn't there
you're the reader and the writer
the crowd's buzz

a sizzly shifting block of midges
as I trailed one hand in the Pregel
or trailed it in the Pregolya
a river named during a wet lunch at Potsdam
sugar furs saltfish copper sandstone corn
so many commodities things being moved
through the Holy Roman Empire of the German Nation
hard to tell what would happen
as the Empire burst like a bag
and logs slipped downriver
to the papermills at Königsberg

how many years back were Slavata and Martinitz
pushed out of that window?
at what hour of the night was it in Ruzyn
or Hradčany Castle they hanged Slansky?
thousands of statements dropped from the presses
and the day I read Kant's starry sentence
on a bronze tablet in Kaliningrad
my protestant faith in the printed text
turned back on itself

Tilly Wallenstein the spider Spinola
Gustavus Ferdinand Charles
Colonel Horn working the Lauterbach Valley
how scrupulous the sense of landscape is
in every description of armies before a battle

the flat sandy soil scrubby woods holm oak and larch
the narrow marshy streams slick oily water
between Rocroy and Rumigny
the lagoons and salt marshes of East Prussia

Simon I sometimes believe it's us poor saps
gives each of these places its strange and exact presence
as if we're part of the action though the whole bloody mess
it doesn't depend on our minds just
for the chosen ground is always packed
with skulls in section norns some end result

*

we cracked too many bottles
in our fuggy bower
we smoked and made mantalk in the small hours
we cut our girls' names on pumpkins and melons
– *Arsille Rosita Emilie*
the letters distorted as they grew
and our writing stopped being ours

cucumber leaves furred with wee spines
like glasspaper or emery skins
you could polish furniture with the dry ones
or stroke your finger over their crinkly pumice
I imagined marketing them like poems
each one the slow rub of high culture
waxing a chairback's wooden pelvis

so I dreamed and wanked in a cage of swelling vegetables
each living graffito mocking my prick's ikons
riverboats passed trailing music like vines
each name went its own way left me behind
the place is a wreck now I just hurry past it
looking for signs of age in myself the used voice
the creased pouchy face on a coathanger
understudy for that weddingcake left out in the rain

half truths cagey handshakes those lyrics written
to your own sadness and tight esteem
I cling to my friends like soft rain on bar windows
I don't believe God is much interested
in this or that country what happens or doesn't
and after twenty odd years breaking lives like firewood
is there anything can shock us now?
the Virgin of Magdeburg charred in a ditch
the sleeping girl they shot because she married out
why give a shit if what you write doesn't last?
could you feel could you really feel any joy
watching the nation states rising up like maggots?

*

the West's last thinker part woodcutter
and part charlatan
is digging trenches on the Rhine
          – lonely uncanny violent
          the artist and the leader
          without expedients
          *apolis*
          without structure and order
          among all that is –
in the summer of '44
a memo named me the most expendable
member of my university

I was thankful digging
*this will be useful to me*
*like an alibi*
I was thinkful dagging
*in the firebreak*
*the firebreak between armed forests*

55

*Herr Professor*
*must keep his head down*
          – bridge and hangar
          stadium and factory
          are buildings
          but they're not dwellings
          *Bahnhof und Autobahn*
          *Staudamm und Markthalle*
          *sind Bauten*
          *aber keine Wohnungen –*
if I refused to drop
three Jews from the faculty
had I not praised
*Totenbaum*
rooftree
coffin
tree of the dead
– a farmhouse in the Black Forest
built two centuries back
by the dwelling of peasants?
as I praised the Führer
it was like all the dead feet
walked into our room
where my wife stood by the fire
cleaning my hairbrush
and I complained to her
about that thin singed aftersmell
its bony frazzle and suddenness
like blotting the word *think*

                    *

he digs deep in the earth
or stands with small tight goggles against the snowglare

a survivor like you and me
outside the ski hut at Todtnauberg
this old smooth fuck
tried stare through history
at the very worst moment

> *Simplex watched the committee men*
> *Shuffle, mumble and give in.*

without conscience
the day they buried Husserl's ashes
I kept to a ribbed path
and listened to the forest
its silent tidal boom
the all cave of language
and I heard him
Masaryk's teacher
as I watched the Rhine
'a wordy digger
is not the worthy digger
of his own grave
you're one of those small fry
who funked my sickroom'
days after he died
I'd written Frau Husserl
'forgive me
I should have stated
my admiration and my gratitude'
then I dropped the dedication
*Sein und Zeit*
was as clean as its title
a set text
the pages resinous
as pine laths

knocked into a box
and the missing name of Edmund Husserl
rosepink like a knot
or the eye of a white mouse

this red Rhine clay
lignite and gravel
*Grund*
I stood on the wet
ontic particles
my boots sogged
in muddy water
fires luffed
on the other bank
fires the French had lit
I bribed a guard
and had six nights
on a mudbank in a *toten Arm*
one hour before dawn
on day seven
I crossed their lines
coffee and a visa
Bolivia Paraguay anyplace
what wouldn't I have given
for just those two things?
but the lieutenant's face
was the face of a student
tensing in a seminar
*der kleine Judenbube*
from NYU

'Go chew acorns
Mr Heidegger

you went with the Nazis'
thrown into a place
unstable here and nowness
a forest pope who lived
on the quiet side of the stink
I answer
*if others did worse*
*they did worse*
*but some felt guilt*
*guilt is not my subject*

male corpses
floating downriver
in white winter battledress
the wide melting root
of Germany
they weren't my fault
one hundred metres of piano wire
the July plotters
noosed in a warehouse
I might've sat in that courtroom
next Helmut Schmidt
a uniformed observer
postponing speech

I was watching the Rhine
as a sealed truck
powered by wood gas
jupped through the forest
I never saw it
nudge the gates of Flossenbürg
never watched them
take that pastor to the gallows

Bonhoeffer Bonhoeffer
is this then *meine Schuld*?

*

> *Simplex sees the final strike*
> *Devastate that evil Reich.*
> *Simplex says I'm going now*
> *You can read this anyhow.*

*

water's twisting down the hillsides in long sheets
all I can say is they fought over the same places
    Alpine passes
    Rhine crossings
    Regensburg bridgehead
    Magdeburg bridgehead
    the plains of Leipzig and Brabant

easy to say it now the war's long over
but you'll find me Simon an idea only
where five khaki caravans are parked on a heath

I'll follow in the Field Marshal's shadow
an orderly an illusion that crosses
ling tyretracks crushed grass
to feel in the left pouch of its battledress
for a pen that'll pass like a baton
from one officer to the next

we unfold ten chairs and a table
in the shabby tent by the flagpole
it's inside/outside
chill temporary
like a field latrine

60

he keeps their delegation waiting
then draws them up
under the Union Jack
tying back a flap
I notice three brown buds on a twig
all gummy and glycerine

von Friedeburg their naval commander
he wept during lunch I wiped glasses
and held them up to the canvas light
they signed the instrument of surrender
then lit cigarettes the way young people used to
after sex in the daytime

                    *

now I can get born again
as a square of tracing paper
in A B or C block
flats brickfields cindertracks
it's 9 a.m.
some Monday in February
a building by a muddy river
on a postwar island

onestorey partitioned
tacked out of hardboard
and scrap fuselage
this aluminum school
is split in four sections

lines radiate
in from each pupil
and one tight thread

links *Lüneburger Heide*
to the Clogher Valley
– provincial world history
or the seedbed of soldiers

*Dill Alexander*
*Montgomery Alanbrooke*
they're crimped on my brain tissue
like patents or postcodes
their building's the hard rectangle
that kitted me out first
as a blue British citizen

which signifies only
that this flattened trashcan
has more than enough room
for Tommy's wee collection
of aesthetic judgements
decals
further descriptions
loony tunes
or Free State referenda

so in all this melt
of incident and hot metal
there's still time to stop over
on the road to Damascus
– a light a voice patch of stamped earth
and if you ask my opinion now
I'll tell you about our musical *Kürbishütte*
then hand you a cucumber
and say it doesn't exist

# Piano Practice
## (Rilke)

Her cotton dress smells like fresh bread
but it's messy with flies this hot afternoon
as she pushes and pulls an étude
to its foregone conclusion

she wants the real thing today
or tomorrow – maybe it's waiting
for her there in the park already?
spoilt is how the bushes and trees are looking

she breaks off clasps her hands and stares through the
    window
a tall window it's heavy with ownership
– she wants to sink into a book but a smell blows
in – it's jasmine – she makes a face and plups her lips

# Date of Renewal
### (Mallarmé)


Snotty spring it's seen off winter
– broken it up like brittle toffee
and made my blues deeper
more lonesome ack even scruffier

so I reheat dawn and dusk in
an old saucepan grey as a gravestone
and chase my dream of pure rhyme
through fields where sap gets right under my skin

then the smell of those trees like sweaty armpits
bores me solid till my dream drops
onto the warm soil that breeds lilacs

I'm a waster my boredom never stops
– no you'll not find me hurrying on
clear skies at the scrake of dawn

# A Nation, Yet Again
(Pushkin)

That kitsch lumber-room is stacked
with a Parnassian dialect:
'love, hope, and quiet reputation
kissed us for a short season
and the gamey letters that we swopped,
in clipped verse, soon had to stop.'
No one, then, praised either side,
though some dipped down among the shades
to find Aeneas and to file
a delicate, a tough, new style
that draws the language to the light
and purifies its tribal rites.
I'm tense now: talk of sharing power,
prophecies of civil war,
new reasons for a secular
mode of voicing the word *nation*
set us on edge, this generation,
and force the poet to play traitor
or act the half-sure legislator.
No matter; there's a classic form
that's in our minds, that makes me warm
to better, raise, build up, refine
whatever gabbles without discipline:
see, it takes me now, these hands stir
to bind the northern to the southern stars.

# Chucking it Away
## (Heine)


I'd a homeland at one time
– strange you weren't born there
and though the trees in it were few and far between
– great parks of chestnuts in Yorkshire
I fell in love with bareness wetness speech
the hazel the holm oak and the screggy hawthorn
(there was a rumour some hardriding junkers
had burnt or felled the trees to stretch their estates
and then one night I was eighteen hitching through Europe
I was taken down the autobahn into the Black Forest
the dark was packed with something I felt shit scared
something I'd no name for but it sickened me)
I was born in the Jewish quarter of a big ugly city
on the other island
and now I live just down the road from all those moors and
    wrecked factories
– it's two nations this place you can't feel easy
though when I drive north up the A1
I find in myself a drab liking for all the poplars and diners
the windsocks and pocked hangars on the airfields
but when my kids pin a map of Ireland in their room
or sit crosslegged under a portrait of Guru Nanak
I'm twinged by different musics
– it's one thing being British
but you need a white skin to be English
then you can shout things in public places
at kids of a different complexion
and feel rooted or threatened or part of the land

while the rest of us keep our heads down feel grateful or
    angry
– as to being Irish I'd like to believe
it's only the difference
between calling yourself James instead of Philip
if your name happens to be Larkin

# The Road to Inver
(Pessoa)

*for Xon de Ros and Jamie McKendrick*

I left a village called Tempo
oh maybe an hour back
and now I'm driving to Inver
in an old beatup gunked Toyota
I've borrowed from a mate in Belfast
(there was a poet down south
who blessed all the new Toyotas in Ireland
– everyone else was driving in circles
but he came out with a firm line
and drove it straight home)

cold as a hub cap
there's a full moon shining
over the pine plantation
that belongs here really
no more than I do
though man and boy I've watched it grow
from naked wee saplings
to mature slightly sinister trees
just as I've watched them bed
two salmon farms and an oyster
farm out there in the bay
(if it was daylight I'd point to
a spot on the ocean that's corrugated
and rusted like scrap metal or
– same thing – a tank trap at high tide)
but it looks like I'm on another journey
in another time

where I go on – go on and on –
without ever having left Belfast
or having to go to Inver
– in Irish it means *river
mouth* – which is a bit like not having read
– I don't know the language –
like not having read
that book – is it a novel or memoir? –
called *The House at Inver*
which stood somewhere on the shelves
in our house in Belfast
which reminds me my grandmother's house
in Belfast was called *Invergowrie*
after the village in the Lowlands she was born in
or maybe that her family came from
(they brought the bronze nameplate with them
when they moved from Glasgow
and settled – more or less – in Ireland)

I'm going to spend the night in Inver
– check in to some B&B
because I can't stay in Belfast
but when I get to Inver I'll be sorry
I didn't stay behind in Belfast
– always this disquiet – I'm anxious
– anxious to no purpose–
always always always
and always too much – over the top –
and all for nothing
on the road to Inver
it's a dream road this
the same road that leads
to the Elver Inn on Lough Neagh

– 's just a phrase *dream road*
like *the rood of time*
or *the long road to nowhere*
or *big fat pursy toad*

the wheel of my borrowed car
is taut like a fishing line
or like reins
and the wheels they go smoothly
over the tired the humpy
old road
that feels a bit like a bog road
– I smile at this symbol as I recall it
and make a right turn
– how many borrowed things do
I go about in or use all day?
but the things that are lent I take
them over and make them mine
– one day way back they even loaned me me
– I'd stake my life on that
though the idea cuts me like a knife
(I feel like – well
a double agent who might be triple)

there's a mobile home by the roadside
– one with no wheels I often used dream of
when my heart and my spirit they
felt cut to pieces as I worried
what would happen my children
– the headlights catch its fence
that's new gardencentre wattle
an open field and the moon
making it cold like bare metal

for the car in which – leaving Tempo –
I felt like a freedom rider
has boxed me in
it's like I'm trapped inside her
and can only control – well the thing –
if I'm locked in it
and feel the car's part of me
I guess they're happy in that stretched
caravan but if they saw me driving past
they'd say *there goes a happy fella*
*he doesn't give a damn what his car looks like*
*no one's ever asked him to write a poem*
*in praise of its make and makers*
– they'd say that of course
if they could see the state this
what they call a *cyar* is in
but none of them would know
that on the road to Inver
in moonlight in my own so
deepdown sadness driving this borrowed
Toyota disconsolately
I'm losing myself in the road in front of me
I'm adding myself to the distance
and then suddenly
out of some terrible desire
I put my foot down and wham forward
but my heart stays with that pile of stones
I swerved past without seeing
– it stood at the wattle gate
a pile of road metal
– yes my heart is empty
my unsatisfied heart
my heart more human than I am and so

much more exact than life is
on the road to Inver near midnight
at the wheel under the moon's light
on the road to Inver – oh
how tiring one's imagination is
on the road to Inver always closer
to Inver – I want to reach out and touch it
like the rocks round Bantry Bay
on the road to Inver
craving peace its slow so slow
drop into our laps but as far
from it and myself as ever

# March, 1941
(Akhmatova)


A sundial on the Menshikov House
a boat makes a stir as it passes
there's nothing no nothing more familiar
to me than the cool glaze of the spires
lying flat out on the water
– that backstreet it's tight like a mousehole
the sparrows might be grey mice on the wires
I mind walks here way back
and this salty taste? I feel it rising from my
    stomach
ack it might not mean disaster

# Table
## (Apollinaire)

My oblong table has round corners. I sit with my boots off, smoking a pipe even though tobacco disgusts me – still its smouldering bitter shag gives me pleasure. Though I wanted to get down to some work this morning, all I've done is shuffle through a few tired-looking drafts. Those gadgets with blotting paper fixed to them are useless – it's better to dry each ripe, each blooded line with unmounted paper. Unmounted is best. Pink like a powdered face, it turns black little by little, till there's a square at the centre, like a dirty bandage. I'm doing nothing right now except describe what's in front of my eyes – that crumpled handkerchief near my right hand, loyal but beaten I want to say, except such a quality isn't visible, isn't seen. There's also a box of Swedish matches upside down, a dullish pink box with a red circle and an A an M a C below a burning torch. It reminds me of railway posters – the last time I went on a train they were the big event. I loved them every bit as much as the buzz and hum deep inside the telegraph poles along the roads where I walked all day.

```
          A
     T         T
          E
     N         T
     I    O    N
```

DANGER DE MORT

74

That was printed on each pole, more exciting than a playbill.

I'm bored. I'm going to snap a clay pipe in two – a wick one – which is really daft. I'll also have to chuck out a few old briar pipes which have got altogether too gummed up, too sticky. Then trying to think about several different things at the same time – a pain in my neck, my eyes gone blank – I shall pluck all the hairs from my fingers. If there's blood, I'll suck each finger until nightfall. Then I'll get up, grope for the matches, light my lamp and write way beyond midnight.

# Paris Ink Sketch

(Verlaine)

Scrubbed like a bartop the roofs look tin
or moony zinc – upended – all angles
like baths and sinks in a plumber's merchants
while out of pointy pencil chimneys
smoke – sinless – scribbles its 5s

the sky's grey – an echo – an encore
like a weepy bassoon
till a stinking tomcat nesh and mangy
screeches strangely
– a cry that's kinked like catgut really

me I walk the streets dreaming of Plato and Phidias
Oedipus and the Sphinx
– those thinking Greeks their forms ideas!
under the blinking eye of these blue gas lamps
these burning beaks

## Winds and Rivers
(from *Prometheus Bound*)


Winds and rivers,
light, sea, earth, winds,
wind on the needlegrass
and light,
light on the greased eel and the greyhound,
I call on you –
on the pure and the slimy,
the running, shotsilk
skim of you –
I call on you as witnesses
to my first millennium
as Zeus's prisoner.
Didn't I make things happen?
Didn't I seize the fire of ideas
and make them leap, tear, fly, sing –
the rush and whap of them
in each split moment! –
and now I can do nothing,
nothing will happen.
Mortal, ashamed, cowed, frightened –
clamped to its frozen edges,
the humans hugged the earth
and waited for wipe-out.
The secret source of fire and heat –
that one, primal,
Idea of all ideas,
I searched it out –
so delicate and brittle

I hid it in a cusp of fennel,
a single spark
inside that aromatic
greeny-white bulb.
I swam like a mullet
with a hook bedded
in its soft mouth –
I swam
in the smell of the ocean,
in the huge dazzle of all ideas
and always hearing
just as I'm hearing now
the quick fluster of seabirds flying.

# Prometheus on Mythology
(from *Prometheus Bound*)

The gods of our new mythology are all generals and politicians. I helped them get power. I watched them drive in stretched limos to ceremonies where they made speeches and then awarded each other honours, titles, medals, stars, brownie points. And always there was some historian handling the press. Down on the ground the people humped heavy loads and suffered back pains and self-disgust. Those humans drudged. They'd no idea what they were for. Witless, glum, trapped, they blundered about with their heads down. So I gave them the idea of skill – first the deftness of hands working, then the techne of making objects out of wood, clay, stone and bone. Then the smelt of soft and tough metals, until they could find in the glow of fire what came first and before all these new arts – the idea of mind. All I felt was an immense patience and good will. Toward everything human I felt friendly. There was nothing alien or strange about the small gnarled artefacts they began to skrimshander out of whalebone, teak, black soapstone. Little gods, animals kissing, keepsakes, bison running, white horses – they began to make images and objects, each with its own aura. When first they started they had eyes but didn't yet know how to look at the world. Their ears were blocked with wax and ignorance, lies that had been stuffed there. I taught them different. They lived in holes and grim caves, not knowing how to build houses or even make bricks. Time and the seasons, the movement of stars and planets, they could measure none of these things. The abstract beauty of pure number, the designing of signs on clay, then paper, the infinite accounts in memory banks – they knew nothing of these. I taught them to sail, fly, glide and push themselves out at the stars – but look at me, stuck here, I can't escape. I was free to refuse my talents, but I gave them, gave them generously.

# Sentence Sound
## (Leopardi)


When I was young – about fifteen or so –
five or six pages in a Fontana paperback
on how the ear
is the only true reader
the only true writer
took me into that uncurtained attic
dedicated to the muse
– here poems are often put together
out of fricatives labials and peachy vowels
here prose is stretched or polished
so it doesn't try imitate
the clearness of that blank windowpane
– and because I was taken to this attic
I admired the workbench its wood
all thick and pitted used but sort of raw
like a floor joist or a railway sleeper
– I admired too
the drills gimlets bradawls hammers punches
even though in more than an hour's searching
I couldn't find a single file
– I searched and searched
missing the raspy texture of the thing
until I lifted a long metal tongue
worn quite smooth out of the wastebin
– I licked – no lisped – that smooth file
till it tasted like either hand of a stopped clock

# Roman Elegy
### (Goethe)

Light through peach blossom
all the while a cat licks
the smoky bust of Medusa on the dressingtable
its tongue raspy
on the greasy marble
the bed bouncy and springy *crik! crik!*
as its deepness stretches and strains
like a swaying bush
or a hawk stooping again and again
into a spongy lush
warm marsh
– let me not be drained
not yet
let the nub
and rod of my great tool
be every which way
stubborn as a mule
while Ermione's ample
Roman bosom and body
lie under barbarian rule

# Souvenir of Manchester
## (Verlaine)

To Theodore C. London

No I haven't seen Manchester
– all that I have seen is one little corner
of Salford but badly narrowly
in spite of fog and streets with no cabs – dirty
streets that didn't help my bad leg
and my two club feet – but my spirits don't sag
under the weight of the memories
– happy memories – I now carry
of this town they call *industrial*
and despite that so very intellectual
niche I occupy maybe it would've been better
if I'd really strutted my stuff – this letter's
naïve sure but picture the elite of Manchester
below me as I lean on the lectern
and they applaud in Paul Verlaine
our rigorous Racine
even while I make it clear
that the true God is Shakespeare

# Inscription for the Tomb of the Painter
## Henri Rousseau the Douanier
### (Apollinaire)

*for Stuart Bell*

Dear douce Rousseau
you can hear us now
can hear us say *hello*!
– Delaunay his wife Monsieur Queval and me
please let our luggage pass freely
through the heavenly gate
where you cast an eye
on each valise
– we'll bring you brushes colours canvases
so that once again
you can be a Sunday painter
an eternal Sunday painter
– one Sabbath you painted my portrait
on another you brushed
the mothy faces of the stars

## *from* Landsflykt
(Strindberg)


I heard a voice out of Europe
a southern accent
– Away to hell, England,
you're so dry on the outside
dry and chalky
but your inside's like a coal barge
parked between the North Sea and the Atlantic
an island of warehouses and corner shops
– they all smell of bacon and stale bread
down with Disraeli
damn the Anglican Church
damn your pious women
who knit and make tea
damn your imperial males
all sabres and pricks
your cheapo novels your daily Godawful papers
your mission halls and Salvation Army

Then I answered out of the North
you're all beef, sin, coal, chalk
but that's no matter
don't think I'm taken in
by your lovely bottles of Pale Ale
your neat warm pubs
or your excellent razor blades
– no, I forgive you
I forgive your crimes in Africa, India, Ireland

– I'm letting you off the hook, Albion,
not for your own sake, never,
but because out of your steam presses
shot Dickens, Darwin, Spencer and Mill!

# The Swan
## (Rilke)


A drudge on piecework cackfooted he bumbles clumsily
on the solid ground a plodder – wally – 's a lunkhead
who wouldn't know a telos if he touched it
trapped in this adhocery – a lame Lockean – he's like
the number thirteen uncomfortable thrawn a misfit
or like a man who leaves behind – being nearly dead –
all the bits and pieces that made up his life

at high tide he quits dry land and breasts the estuary
– glad to bear its weight it receives him with a sigh
all those ripples algebra pure sequences that mean
himself alone a silent swan secure and sovereign
– an ark with wings for sails then a sovereign harp whose
new strings ripple like reeds
as it rides its moment

# The Owls
(Baudelaire)


Owls perch in yew trees like strange gods
their eyes glauque but open as they meditate
– they don't budge until dusk has tamped down
the sun below the horizon

then they feed us this little scrap of wisdom
– *where there's only one game in town*
*that game is best avoided*
and then they add *it's late* – maybe they mean *too late*?

# Prometheus' Last Speech
## (from *Prometheus Bound*)

Holy Mother, Themis, Earth,
it must all break
here in this wet yard
at the world's end
where they design pain
in secret for me
and cross my name –
my whole nature out –
by writing *REBEL*
then mocking me for what I'm not.
Men, women, tiny kids,
every juicy little life –
Zeus wanted crush them.
I heard their stittering,
their frantic cries,
cries like pebbles bouncing
on a stone floor,
and my conviction
was simple and complete.
That's why I stole
that restless, bursting,
tight germ of fire,
and chucked its flames
like a splatter of raw paint
against his state.
They seized the running trails
and ran with them,
every mind fizzing like resin –

racing, dancing, leaping free,
jumping up into the sky,
and nudging deep
into the ocean's bottom.
Every mind was a splinter
of sharp, pure fire
that needled him
and made him rock
uneasy on his throne.
See Zeus, shaken
as these new lights burn
and melt his walls.
Let Prometheus go out
and become one
with the democratic light!

# The Briar
(Baudelaire)


An author owns me – I'm his pipe
my complexion it's coalblack – collied – like that
of a slavegirl he's rescued but I'm glad to let
him believe this as with one feely finger he tamps in the shag

when he's really sad I'm like a thatched
cabin with smoke rising from its chimney
– his missus is cooking a heavy supper
for the ploughman slumped on the settle

I tie up his soul and stroke it softly
in the silky blue net
that curls up from my hot lips

the rings I make are so so balmy
they soothe his heart and his spirit
then the poor man doesn't he start to feel happy?

# The Crate
(Ponge)

Half-way between a cage and a cell, the French language has *crate*, a simple latticed box dedicated to preserving fruits that are tainted by the slightest suffocation.

Put together in a manner that allows it to be easily taken apart when its task is completed, it is never used twice. Also it lasts even less time than the melting or cloudy foodstuffs it contains.

At every corner of those streets that end in marketplaces, it shines with the unselfconscious purity of fresh white wood. Still completely new, and slightly stunned to be in a clumsy pose in a network of streets that always get left behind, this object is surely one of the most sympathetic – it's not a good idea to dwell on its fate for very long.

# The Orange
(Ponge)

Just like a sponge, an orange always aspires to return to its original shape after it has gone through the ordeal of being squeezed. But where a sponge always succeeds, an orange never does. Its cells are crushed, its tissues torn. Only the skin, thanks to its elasticity, creeps softly back into shape, as an amber liquid spreads – it has a sweet, refreshing scent, for sure, but one which carries with it a bitter consciousness of prematurely expelled pips.

Must one take sides over these two ways of timidly supporting heavy-handed pressure? – the sponge is nothing but muscle, and stuffs itself with wind, or with clean or dirty water. It's an ungainly athlete. The orange has better taste, except it's too passive – and this perfumed sacrifice . . . really it gives the oppressor too much credit.

But it's not enough to have recalled the orange's particular habit of refreshing the air and delighting its executioner. One must stress the liquid's glorious colour – better than lemon juice, it obliges the larynx to open wide in order to pronounce the word, as though it's swallowing juice with no curling of the upper lip, no ruffling of its whiskers.

For the rest, one remains lost for words to express the admiration which this envelope deserves – the soft pink oval and fragile glass in this thick warm blotter whose extremely thin but pigmented skin – it's sourly sapid – is just rough enough for the light to catch the fruit's perfect form in a dignified manner.

But at the end of this really rather too brief study – it's been carried out as promptly as possible – one must pick up the pip. This grain, shaped like a miniature lemon, also shows the white wood of the lemon tree on its exterior, while its interior is either peagreen or a soft seed. After the Chinese lantern's sensational explosion of flavours, colours, scents, it's this which constitutes the fruity glass itself – the relative duration and the greenness (not always entirely insipid) of wood, branch, leaves, which is the tiny sum that adds up to the fruit's reason for existing.

# Horse Chestnuts
(Goethe)


Chestnuts ripen – spiky a bit like traps
then their shells split open
and then or before that they fall to the ground
the first one I ever – age five – saw
lying in my grandmother's garden
I thought it a small glossy brown
– brown and raw – dog turd
and progged it with a stick
it was hard but it wasn't crap
and almost I thought enjoyed being rubbed
in the palm of my hand
just as likewise – a long time later –
I'd rub a drop of amber
before placing my hand on your lap

# Creation and Animation
(Goethe)


One time Jack Adam was a mucky clot
or clod God shaped into a human
– from out his mother's womb he dragged
all kinds of dreck and grot

but Elohim blew into his nose
the most beautiful soft breezes
– he stood up then erect and tall
and let out huge snottery sneezes

bigboned smoothmembered handsome head
he was often dull and gloomy
till Noah handed him a foamy
big chirpy pewter tankard

the putz of course begins to rise
when the liquid meets his lips
hits his stomach and then fires
his blood like warm – like yeasty dough

so Hafiz know your every lyric
and your own godlike example
will raise and ring full pentup glasses
to the great creator's temple

# The Wait
### (Khazendar)

If you sit here
you'll see his face quite clearly
a spring in his step but his face
dead pale like a thorn
– a long slender one from a boxthorn
he'll sit at the table yes
but he'll keep in shadow
and appear smaller than he was before
– coffee a glass of water
they'll sit there and wait
– wait for ages
the coffee'll go cold
and the water'll get warm
don't think he's a stone
bare and unfletched
a figure with no face
– one that doesn't quiver
it's just that the light's gone
and dropped him in a deep pit
(he's been in the blockhouse)
– maybe an hour later
he takes a sip and winces
– tepid water
he slits a smile like a paperknife
you'll see such a smile
only once in your life

now they'll crowd the light
and poke about in his darkness
– to them it's a puzzle
though they can tell that in spirit
he's gone out the door

# A Single Weather
(Khazendar)


They've got gaps in them the best walls
– it was a geg the way we'd grip hands
then slip through that tall – tall
and tight – gap in the wall
yes we squinched through that fissure
came back again and again we did
under fruit that was fit to burst

I could hear you trapped in your own voice
as we made sleaked talk – worse and worse –
by a well that since we were kids
no one'd drawn a bucket from ever
– unlike the sky you were never the same
and come nightfall you were different again
you felt no right to go back – both it
and the will to return
you'd let them slip

# Une Rue Solitaire
## An Epilogue

You find the poem's title
but not the poem
– maybe it does exist so you can try till
the what's-it? of dawn – till dayclean –
– try write it out in your own form
of this language? – its rhythm
claggy and neoneo
classical like the buildings and walls
in a painting by De Chirico
or this phrase you maybe lifted
from some livre de poche
– nous prenons
la route qui mène à Inver
(a narrow a rough road
not bog or famine quite
it leads this road
back to the Elver Inn on Lough Neagh)
or else it's some phrase you want
to fold up like a pastrycook
– fold it in four
clean little lines
of makeshift verse –
il court au jardin
et s'échappe par une porte
qui donnait
sur une rue solitaire
and though you like the low tidal
the neap dryness in *a deserted street*

it's not – nay never – no not at all
what you want to say
so you go right back to that *rue solitaire*
where you maybe find Onan
– is he named for a port? –
trying to cast his seed
– et tais toi! says the sun le sol-
eil whose light's shut up in a one
way street you squeak down
the wrong way – which again isn't
in this onehorse town
quite what you want to say

# Note

## 'The Caravans on Lüneburg Heath'

Simon Dach (1605–59) was professor of poetry in Königsberg and the most important figure in the Königsberg circle of poets. His poem, 'Klage über den endlichen Untergang und Ruinirung der Musicalischen Kürbs-Hütte und Gärtchens. 13 Jan. 1641', was first published in 1936. It is printed in the selection of seventeenth-century poems in Günter Grass's novella, *Das Treffen in Telgte*, which is set near the end of the Thirty Years War. 'The Caravans on Lüneburg Heath' is loosely based on Simon Dach's 'Lament over the Final Demise and Ruination of the Musical "Pumpkin Hut" and the Little Garden' and is also indebted to *The Meeting at Telgte*, Ralph Mannheim's translation of Grass's novella. Mannheim translates 'Kürbs-Hütte' as 'Cucumber Lodge/Bower' and notes the allusion to Isaiah 1:8 – 'And the daughter of Zion is left as a cottage in a vineyard, as a lodge in a garden of cucumbers, as a besieged city.' Mannheim also explains that Cucumber Lodge was an informal Königsberg literary society which used to meet in the poet Heinrich Albert's garden in a bower overgrown with cucumbers. There they would sing their own songs set to music by Albert.

I have also drawn on various essays by Martin Heidegger and on certain evasive, and probably mendacious, public statements which Heidegger issued in order to justify his conduct under the Nazi regime. I have drawn, too, on Paul Celan's poem to Heidegger, 'Todtnauberg'.